Trust and Live Without Panic

Silvia Araya

Translation: Paulo Porras S.

BALBOA.
PRESS
A DIVISION OF HAY HOUSE

ISBN: 978-1-4525-5554-6 (sc)
ISBN: 978-1-4525-5553-9 (e)

Balboa Press books may be ordered through booksellers or by contacting:
Balboa Press
A Division of Hay House
1663 Liberty Drive
Bloomington, IN 47403
www.balboapress.com
1-(877) 407-4847

Because of the dynamic nature of the Internet, any web addresses or
links contained in this book may have changed since publication and
may no longer be valid. The views expressed in this work are solely those
of the author and do not necessarily reflect the views of the publisher,
and the publisher hereby disclaims any responsibility for them.

The author of this book does not dispense medical advice or prescribe the use
of any technique as a form of treatment for physical, emotional, or medical
problems without the advice of a physician, either directly or indirectly. The
intent of the author is only to offer information of a general nature to help
you in your quest for emotional and spiritual well-being. In the event you use
any of the information in this book for yourself, which is your constitutional
right, the author and the publisher assume no responsibility for your actions.

Any people depicted in stock imagery provided by Thinkstock are
models, and such images are being used for illustrative purposes only.
Certain stock imagery © Thinkstock.

Illustrations by Cristina Gonzalez and Maria Judit Rodriguez

Printed in the United States of America
Balboa Press rev. date: 8/7/2012

Acknowledgments

First of all, I would like to thank God for his unconditional love; for making me an instrument of his by giving me the drive and the words to write this book.

To my parents, my sister, and my nephew for their support and love.

To my aunt Norma, for her wisdom, tenderness, and devotion to others. Also, for her help in making this book even better

I would also like to thank:

Doreen Virtue
Wayne W. Dyer
Collette Baron-Reid
Iyanla Vanzant
Deepak Chopra
And
Louise Hay

Thank you for inspiring me every day with your
teachings and your works

Contents

Acknowledgments   v
Preface   1
Introduction   5
Panic Attacks Are Just Reactions   11
How is it Born?   15
Fear of Death: Guilt, Punishment, and God   21
Control   29
Secondary Winnings   35
Symptoms: Why Panic Attacks?   41
Faith   47
You Are the Only One Who Will Always Be There   55
Finding the Blessings in Every Situation   63
Techniques   69
Final Notes   81

Preface

Panic attacks are more common than they are thought to be. Millions of people suffer from them every day and they don't even know it.

The numbers are high, but I suspect they may be even higher. Many ignore the name of what they suffer from, because they mistake it for other diseases, or because they feel too embarrassed to seek help or to find out what it is they actually endure. Others do know but feel ashamed to admit it and remain, just like the former, outside of the world statistics.

Many of these people suffer in silence, for they fear what others may think of them when they tell someone else, especially their family and friends; therefore, they fail to receive psychological or spiritual treatment or support.

Several investigations confirm my hypothesis that the phenomenon is increasingly frequent due to the fast-tracked lifestyle we carry on, jobs that require "the ability to work under pressure", mass dismissals, the extinction of some sectors of the economy. We get constantly bombarded by the media on "how bad the world is doing", the decay of the environment, food and water shortages, deaths on the news round the clock, natural disasters, and much more.

So many people experience these painful situations nowadays, the anxiety and stress levels are higher than ever. People are running all the time and they don't really know where they want to go; they look and look but not in the right places.

It's time to look back inside ourselves and remember who we really are: light and love.

With this little book, I would like to take you to the journey I had to make through very dark places, in order to understand all of those who are passing through those gloomy caves as well.

At the end of the tunnel I saw the light clearer than ever, and everything I needed came to me effortlessly.

I hope that my experience helps you find your truth and see panic attacks as a great teacher dressed up in a strange costume.

Namaste!
Silvia
Costa Rica, 2011

*"If you knew Who walks by your side
down this roadThat You have chosen,
feeling fear would be impossible"*

A Course in Miracles

Introduction

It starts without warning and it comes in without permission, without calling. The feeling slowly arrives on its own like a trickle of water and quickly floods like a wave... that January night was darker than other nights, and I went to bed at the usual time unaware of what was coming, with my alarm set, since I had to go to work the next day.

I closed my eyes in the darkness of the room, interrupted only by the glow of the mute TV. A feeling of breathlessness started to press my chest, followed by the beating of my heart, which increased in strength and speed, and thoughts of death filled my head with unstoppable power.

I couldn't believe that I would die on that day, alone in my bed; for I was sure that I wouldn't even have the strength to get up and drive myself to the hospital.

Even when I knew what this was about, every time I had one of these spells it impossible for me to remember that it was just a temporary nightmare.

I shut my eyes even harder and started repeating to myself once and again that what I felt was psychological, that it was going to pass just like the other times, but it wouldn't go away.

I began to cry, feeling impotent; the fear had already dropped the temperature of all my body and I was trembling in spite of the three layers I had on top.

My first impulse was to call my mother, and have her tell me that everything was going to be fine, but it was too late and I didn't want to scare her over "a silly thing" such as this, so I got up on my feet and the anxiety had me walk in circles around the dining table. The feelings wouldn't go away, and without realizing it I was talking to myself, talking out loud to God. Tears were rushing down; my chest was pushing them out.

I moved my arms in strange circles; I couldn't control these movements but they comforted me somehow. I kept walking in circles, talking, moving my arms, and shushing myself to avoid waking someone up.

I knew I had to go to work in a few hours, and that tormented me even more, so I went back to my room but I couldn't sleep. This was the longest spell I had ever had.

At that moment, I decided to overcome my shame and I knocked on my roommate's door, to ask her to sleep with me. Deep inside, I was also hoping that she would comfort me and calm me down, but she went straight to my bed and continued with her sleep.

I was trapped, I didn't feel any better, and now I couldn't turn the TV on, or talk, or cry out loud, for I didn't want to wake her up. I had to find a way to fall asleep as soon as possible.

I tried to put into practice what my mother had taught me about our inner child, and I curled up in a fetal position, I grabbed my pillow as if it were a baby and began to "soothe it" while I sobbed.

The hours went by, and half asleep I could hear the birds singing, revealing the sunrise.

It had been the longest night of my life…

Panic attacks are much more frequent than they are thought to be, and millions suffer from them every day under a shadow of ignorance.

Due to the reality of its symptoms, its diagnosis is very difficult because it can be disguised as different disorders and this makes statistics deceptive.

In the United States, approximately 15 to 19.5% of the population suffers from anxiety attacks in a year, and around 28% suffer from them throughout their lives (González 2009).

Puchol (2003) states that:

"Anxiety Disorders are nowadays considered the most common mental disorder in the United States".

Approximately 2.4 million North Americans between the ages of 18 and 54 – that is, around 1.7% of the population – suffer from Panic Disorder.

As I mentioned previously, these numbers could be higher, given that panic attacks are more common every day, in a population that every day has more anxiety and less faith; also, due to the fact that many think they suffer from a different disease or ignore the real name of their ailment.

A small part of the population that suffers from panic attacks knows that their illness is not physical, but still they are not included in the statistics, and they feel too embarrassed to seek psychological help.

The final element is present in all of us. We let ourselves be affected by what people say when we express that we can't get on an elevator, or when we don't feel like going to a particular place (especially if it's far away from home), or when we are unable to go to the supermarket or ride a bus by ourselves. It affects our self-esteem because many times we feel unable to be "normal" and perform the everyday activities that everybody does without any problem.

These are the reasons why it is very hard to give an exact figure of people who undergo these episodes and that are usually labeled as being *"nervous"*, *"fearfull"*, *"weird"*, *"weak"*…

All these signs motivated me to turn my own experience into a way to speak up regarding this situation that silently lives in many households; perhaps some of the techniques that helped me may be useful to others too.

Throughout this book I will try to use more positive ways to refer to panic attacks, and will try to avoid using the words *problem* or *disease*, since I don't believe that these are what panic attacks are.

Even when they are a mental issue, born from our thoughts, I think it's also important to talk about when these thoughts and beliefs manifest themselves in the physical dimension, in the form of symptoms.

It may happen that when a person with this kind of episodes reaches a hospital, the doctors are unable to determine the cause of the dizziness, the shortness of breath, the chest pains, and so forth, and simply conclude: what you have is *stress*. However, as Doreen Virtue, Ph.D. says, the experience is just like that of a horror movie: the tears are real, the fear is real, THE SYMPTOMS AND THE AILMENT ARE REAL, but what is causing them IS NOT REAL, it's just a movie. This phrase has burned into my head, because only those of us who have experienced an episode know how strong the fear can be felt in our bodies, creating all sorts of chain reactions.

"... so we can confidently say: the Lord is my helper; I will not fear"

Hebrews 13:6

Panic Attacks Are Just Reactions

The title summarizes very well what I have come to discover; that panic crises are due to reactions that may be programmed as well as biological. I would like to focus for the time being on the latter, because it seems to me that the human body is equipped to act in response to dangerous situations. For example, imagine our ancestors in prehistoric times. They knew that when they saw a predator or an enemy tribe coming, they had to run or prepare to defend themselves. Our organism sets off a series of mechanisms, such as increasing the heart rhythm, the breathing rate, the sensation of having to RUN AWAY, adrenalin rushing everywhere, sweating, cortisol, glucagon as a source of energy, sleep and hunger are inhibited. Why? Because there is a threat, and being alert is far more important than anything else at that moment.

Personally, I believe that the unconscious does not distinguish between a visual threat, such as a saber-toothed tiger, or the thought that I am going to die, very common in panic crises. This is why our body prepares in the same way for a real scenario as it does for an imaginary one, and all these physiological reactions are very real, and are part of the symptoms that lead people to think that they are actually going to die.

What is important to acknowledge here is that the feelings are very real, but what created them is not. It's a movie, they are only thoughts, and therefore we can reverse the process and return to a state of calm by simply breathing deeply to decrease our heart rhythm, making the other symptoms disappear, since they are just reactions of this body perfectly created by God.

Talking to oneself in those moments (among other techniques) is fundamental. We can tell ourselves: *everything is fine; there is nothing to worry about; there are no real threats; we are safe; nothing bad is going to happen; you are just scared*. Also, realizing the blessing that this episode means, because the fact that the body responded the way it did (even when it does not match reality) means that there's a part of us that chooses life, that chooses to continue living, and that does not want to abandon this human experience. It is important to acknowledge this, because it would be a problem if we didn't have this instinct for survival.

When we realize that we may have "a more sensitive tonsil" than others, and that our emergency system is working perfectly, we will be able to see that there is really nothing strange, that we are not weird or abnormal, and that we are simply very anxious due to our lack of trust and faith. It means we have to turn the volume down on the thoughts that come with the horror movie playing in our heads; sit down and say: *it's only a movie, it's not real; we are going to be confident that everything is and will be fine.* Faith!

This is when we rule out that the crisis is physiological in origin. It is time to focus on the actual root-cause of the symptoms: the mind.

"There is no separation between God and His creation."

A Course in Miracles

How is it Born?

From my own experience and that of many others I have been able to observe, I see that panic attacks begin to build up in childhood years. At some point, some highly traumatic experience: a death or near-death experience, abuse, an accident, or any difficult situation for a child, in which he or she experiences ABANDONMENT. In other words, if the child believed that he or she had to face a dangerous or frightening experience, and felt (even when not necessarily so) that nobody could comfort or protect him/her in that moment.

For example, my childhood; to me, the most traumatic experience of my early years was an intestine condition I had that forced me to take medication and to have exams of all kinds done to me. This happened when I was between 0 and 3 years old. This problem ended in a very delicate surgery that took over 10 hours, followed by weeks of hospitalization.

Some days later I had to return to the hospital with internal bleeding, which placed me in a dilemma. If they operate on me, I may die. If they don't operate, I may also die.

Miraculously, the bleeding stopped. No further surgery was needed, and I have had no issues ever since.

I can still remember some things, others I can't, but from the pieces I have been able to recall and put together, and from my father's stories, it was a very hard experience on everybody, and even though my parents wanted to be with me all the time, they weren't able to. Many of the experiences, such as the surgery, the exams, and others, I had to endure by myself, and probably with a feeling of indescribable abandonment.

It doesn't matter if the "abandonment" was intentional or not. What matters is that it was real for the child, and this emotion is recreated once and again during the crises. This is why there is no logic to being afraid of riding a bus, or of a family trip, or a store. Or why an adult is scared when facing one of these harmless scenarios; it is precisely because it isn't the adult, but the child inside of us who is scared.

Many times, even our "grown-up" part comes out and scolds our child for having these reactions, or gets angry because it knows that there is nothing to fear. But in these moments we must remember that it's a child who is scared, and ask ourselves: *what would I tell a child if I found him/her in this situation?* Think about it, it's a good exercise. Even when you can't imagine yourself as a child, try picturing any boy or girl, and let yourself act as the loving adult that little person needs in such a moment.

Going back to the trauma or the difficult situations in our childhood, let's not spend any time or energy trying to figure out whose fault it was, why they did it, or why I wasn't comforted in my moments of pain. That is in the past, and there is nothing we can do to change it, except to accept it and to know that experiencing situations like those is part of our learning process. On the other hand, our caretakers did what they could; using the emotional and financial tools they had at hand in those circumstances. They also, probably, bore their own unattended child within themselves. Trying to find whose fault it was, or looking for ways to change the past will only delay the healing process. But I admit that acceptance also takes time.

For some people, crises of this kind persist throughout their lives, but in most cases I know, the episodes cease for some years and may return after a difficult or traumatic experience, such as giving birth, near-death experiences (including serious illness), losing a job, ending a relationship, changes in financial status; any situation that makes the person feel abandoned again, or losing control.

At this point, we often ask ourselves: *What is going on? I used to be able to do these things, and I can't anymore? I used to be "normal", I don't know what happened.* These words are very common because the scared little child is functioning at an unconscious level in many people, so the situation being faced at that moment triggers the feeling of abandonment and neglect that was hidden under the rug for so many years, where *"no one could see it"*, but that was actually always there because it was never healed. The blessing here is that, if this feeling emerges years later, when we have more emotional tools, many of us are adults, fully capable of looking after ourselves, then it is a great opportunity for personal growth.

This is the perfect moment to comfort that little boy or girl that is so scared, and you are the perfect person to do it. We will revisit this subject later on.

"… for He has said: I will never leave you nor forsake you"

Hebrews 13:5

Fear of Death: Guilt, Punishment, and God

common factor in all of us who suffer or have suffered from this condition is fear of death. You must think there is nothing abnormal about this, since we are all somehow afraid of dying; but when it comes to panic attacks, it is different. I am talking about being indescribably terrified of leaving this world. A feeling of desperation and abandonment beyond words; it is feeling the real threat of an inevitable fact, of losing control at that moment and being unable to do anything but wait for it to come. Everyone I know that has these crises suffers from a feeling of constant reluctance to die, even if they haven't recognized it yet.

They feel anguished when they hear about someone – known or stranger – who has passed away or is suffering from a lethal or strange disease. Even hearing about these subjects makes them feel anxious, and can even lead them to a crisis if they haven't learned how to control these thoughts.

This paralyzing feeling sometimes leads the individual to avoiding all sorts of situations that may be considered dangerous; avoiding certain foods, places, trips, and others.

Fear of death may get to control one's life completely and affect all of its dimensions: relationships, family, friends, work, school, recreational activities, and hobbies; without realizing it, little by little the patient shuts him or herself up in a little dark box, to which only he or she holds the key.

I have found this factor in all the panic cases that I have known, to a greater or lesser extent.

This feeling regarding the transition of a living being seems to be only a mistaken idea; in the past, other civilizations experienced the passing of a loved one as a celebration. It was considered an important and joyous occasion for the deceased. At what point did we lose this vision, and why? What keeps us from thinking of this event with joy again? What would happen if we taught future generations to see it in a different way?

This fear is often generalized, and people also develop an aversion to illness, for it represents death and/or suffering. Again, a person will do everything possible to avoid disease, and if s/he ever catches one, it may trigger a panic episode. This condition, called hypochondria in medical and psychological jargon, may complicate the patient's life a little more. It is common that obsessive thoughts and behaviors arise regarding disease, such as constantly checking on the composition and expiration dates of foods, or avoiding certain foods that were taken in the past without a problem, and the individual becomes more and more withdrawn within his/her fear.

If you find yourself in this situation, it is very important to try to stop going down this road as soon as possible, and seek help.

Rejection of death can arise due to various reasons; however, from my mother's observations over years of practicing psychology, I have learned that fear of God and/or guilt is also present in all cases.

Fear of God has been instilled over centuries, and has created in people a feeling of apprehension about being punished. This can have a very deep origin, and many people, due to different circumstances in their lives – especially in their childhood –, reach the conclusion that they are bad or deserve bad things happening to them, and therefore God will punish them for their wrongdoing, or for having "failed to fulfill" His commands. The same thing happens with guilt: those of us who, at some point, come to think that we are not good enough, perfect enough, or beautiful enough, shape the idea that we deserve punishment for "our flaws", and we UNCONSCIOUSLY allow all of our thoughts to be filled with fear. This way, we live our lives according to "what we have earned": punishment.

In the Bible, 1 John 4:18 says that fear bears punishment within itself; this is because just allowing fear in our lives makes us be unaligned or feel separated from our source, the universe, God, or however you want to call it. The Ego ("Edge God Out", as Wayne Dyer calls it) is that part of us where we feel away from God and keeps us from becoming what we really are: love. This situation alone is punishment enough for our soul.

The Ego lives and feeds on fear. It believes in every commandment and belief of this earthly world. Living this way will only makes us feel that we are lacking something, that we are undeserving, and that we need to have control and constant fear.

A person living from Ego will try to avoid rejection, and in the end, that is simply fear. Fear of not being loved or accepted by God, by our parents, by society, by our partner, friends, family… and so we go back to John's quote, which says that "perfect love drives out fear". In this little phrase, we find our solution.

If we are willing to take the longer road, guilt will not have a place in our lives. By "the longer road", I mean forgiving and loving ourselves. If we are able to forgive ourselves, we will realize that there is NOTHING wrong with us, that we have always been and will always be perfect, because we are the image of our origin. And most important, that the "mistakes" we made were the result of our best efforts, with the tools we had with us at the time, as Louise Hay says. Moreover, sometimes we are unaware of the purpose of that situation taking place. We don't know the implication of our words, and in many cases it is important for that moment to happen, for I will learn something from it, or someone else will, and guilt will not fix or change anything. If a ton of guilt or worrying could solve anything, I would tell you, "Go ahead; feel really bad". But we know it doesn't work that way, and guilt will only bring punishment and will not repair anything.

The following picture shows my view of how the whole process of "episodes of less peace" works.

The root of it all is neglect, and sometimes rejection as well. They are both fed by guilt, which in turn holds the top where the symptoms lie.

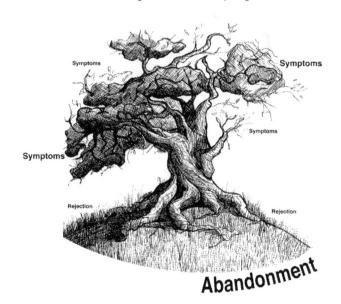

I like to use this picture when I explain that what we normally see are the leaves of the plant or tree, and many spend their lives using resources and energy to treat the top of the tree only. But this is just the symptoms. If we want to make the situation disappear, we must work on the roots, and the leaves will automatically change.

It is also important not to make room for guilt in our lives, as this will only encourage the sense of neglect and rejection that we feel deep inside.

By trimming the tree top, we achieve nothing. The branches will grow back, and many people "trim their tree" with highly addictive, dangerous and expensive medication; or with addictions. Let's focus on the roots and everything will begin to change involuntarily.

"In the spring, the flower fades away while the fruit grows. So will your inner being fade while the divine grows inside of you." (Vivekananda)

Our energies must be focused on perceiving the existence of what we want in our lives, not on what we wish to eliminate. I repeat: our energies must be focused on perceiving the existence of what we want in our lives, not on what we wish to eliminate. The latter will vanish little by little, while love and forgiveness take place inside of us.

I wrote on purpose "the existence of what we want", because everything has already been given to us. We just haven't noticed yet, since we have had our eyes set on what we thought we needed.

"And if we know that he hears us—whatever we ask—we know that we have what we asked of him." (1 John 5:15)

"Give all your worries and cares to the Lord, for He cares about you."

1 Peter 5:7

Control

For all who have trouble regulating their anxiety, there is a matter (or an issue) of control in almost every case. All that anxiety inside our bodies will always search for a way to get out or get reduced in some way. Those of us who experience these panic episodes often live under the illusion of having control of everything that happens inside and outside of us; therefore, when we feel we are losing control, we fall into one of these episodes.

Control is an illusion created by Ego; since it feels we are away from God, it seeks a way of having everything under its control. It is driven by fear: fear of things changing, fear of the unknown, fear of things not working out the way we expect; all this creates more tension and more anxiety, since it is not our natural state. Our natural condition is to trust, to let flow... someone once told me in a dream: "the important thing is to flow".

The control that Ego makes us adopt doesn't really exist because we have no power over the circumstances that surround us; we can only control our thoughts. We can change the way we are affected by different situations in life. Only I decide if what happens at a given moment at work or at home, or what someone may have told me, affects me, offensive as it may have been. We only have control over the decision of whether or not words will offend us, sadden us, or anger us.

Real control is exercised by the Universe and its divine impulse. But it doesn't operate in a human way. It operates from harmony and balance. It doesn't work based on strength, but on the energy under which everything is already arranged, so that every plant, every river, every animal knows exactly what to do. Nobody *pulls* plants up, or *pushes* rivers forward; they just let the divine intelligence flow through them, for they rest confident that there are universal laws behind these processes.

We stopped trusting our source a long time ago, and we began to operate on fear. Without realizing it, we were holding the reins of a horse that never existed, but the illusion somehow comforts us. However, no illusion lasts forever, and when it falls apart, all that is left is fear. The fear that was always hiding behind it all, because we never treated it: we disguised it.

We develop this mechanism at a very early stage, and have it "turned on" for decades. That is why panic episodes often occur right after some crisis or huge change in our lives. In my case, my whole world crumbled before my eyes during a time of financial hardship in my family. I thought I had everything worked out, everything under control. Money was my security. Many people have told me that their triggering point was when they gave birth, or the death of a beloved one, or some other traumatic incident that shook the very floor they were standing on. The problem is that we often stand on a false surface that is just waiting to explode in any moment. It is normal, then, to have a panic reaction after such an incident, but the important thing is to see the opportunity that arises from the rubble; this is the perfect moment to let go of the reins and begin to flow with life, in order to build a floor that we carry within ourselves, and not outside.

What is most important about control is to identify when we are using it and knowing how to let it go. A technique that I recommend is to imagine you are in a restaurant. You choose something from the menu, you tell the waiter, and after that you normally wait sitting at the table. You don't go to the kitchen to tell the chef how he's supposed to chop this or cook that. There is a certain confidence that we will receive what we ordered. The problem is that when you go to the kitchen and snatch that pan from God or the Universe, He respects our decision; He won't say anything and He'll let us have it. Then we will end up exhausted from cooking all that dinner and it probably won't be as we had imagined it. Then, we get angry at God and tell Him: "But you told me to ask, so I did". Yes, but we never let Him act. We wanted to have control at all times. That is why we are not wrong when we ask with all our hearts; we are wrong at the step that follows after that.

In a different scenario, you order and wait patiently, knowing that the order will come in its due time. You imagine all the smells given off by that culinary work of art, and you feel all the taste melting in your mouth. You start enjoying that dish *as if* you already had it before you, because you know it will be there shortly, because you TRUST the cook completely. For this person, not only eating was a wonderful experience, but the wait was just as good. He didn't waste his energy; he simply ALLOWED the process to flow on its own, in a peaceful way.

Control will only bring tension, and in turn this will bring more anxiety, which is equivalent to being a group of volcanoes about to explode into a panic crisis any time.

If you begin to trust in life, that tension will vanish little by little, and you will start noticing it all over your body, for that same insecurity blocks your throat and gives you that choking sensation in those nervous moments. If we let go instead, all our muscles will relax and our blood will be able to flow more easily.

Control is actually in the best of hands, and learning to trust those hands will spare you many episodes of distress.

Don't push the river forward.

"Necessity leads the way to change"

SAV

Secondary Winnings

For a change to take place, the only thing the Universe needs is our willingness. Fifty percent of the job is done just by us being willing to change. The Universe will take care of the other 50%.

I start by stating this fact because many people have the intention to change some situation in their lives, but then they express that after trying for a long time and with different techniques, nothing has changed. They are still in the same place, stuck in the mud.

This situation applies to everything in life, including panic crises. People wonder what are they *not* doing, or what are they doing wrong that doesn't let them change this suffering. One of the reasons might be secondary winnings.

Secondary winnings are benefits that you obtain unconsciously from your situation. Thanks to a depression, a nervous breakdown, financial hardship, or the like, you draw the attention or pity of others. You might be receiving confirmation that you don't deserve what you want. It may even be the perfect excuse to have others take care of your problem, and therefore you postpone taking responsibility and looking after yourself.

For some people, it is one or several of these options. However, it is important not to give in to guilt, for it will only make the little child within us feel bad, and reinforce the condition that created the problem in the first place.

The first step is to understand that all this takes place at an unconscious level, and that it is only an automatic response that tells us we only do what we have learned in our lives. It is also a reflection of our fear of change, and in some cases, fear of being better, because we feel that we don't deserve it.

Whatever the reason may be for the unconscious to act like this, the next step is to realize what kind of belief is holding me back from changing and taking full responsibility of my life.

The benefit (or the winnings), in all cases, is not to change.

In the situation in which a person gets attention, or has someone else take care of his/her life, the key is for that 'someone else' to stop doing the work that the person can do for him or herself.

It may be clearer with an example. Imagine a woman that has suffered from panic attacks for years, and whose family has learned to live with her condition. Her situation has deteriorated so much that she is unable to even go shopping. Her family structure has reorganized in such a way that whenever she needs to buy something, her daughters do it for her.

In the few occasions in which she plucks up courage and leaves the house, she normally suffers a crisis halfway through, and leaves her car abandoned at the place of the event; later, her son has to go to pick up the car and bring it home.

This is a very common situation in which the person has no real need of changing, even though she hates her panic attacks and suffers from them every day, for there is a well-orchestrated organization that surrounds her and makes it unnecessary for her to take care of herself.

In this kind of situation, it is important that the family or any other 'facilitators' step aside, for even when their intentions are good, they are delaying the healing process of their loved one.

We can learn to momentarily let go of these 'winnings' for a greater good that will come later: healing and independence. Knowing that we need no one else but ourselves to go out and feel good at all times will be the reward for letting go of the hidden benefit that we were unaware of.

Remember that love cannot be where there is fear. Give up that fear of change, of taking care of yourself, and you will see there will be nothing but benefits.

After a certain age, it is our turn to become our own parents; this will give us the opportunity of becoming loving parents of ourselves (we will talk about this in another chapter). Don't be afraid; you are fully equipped to take on this task.

As Betty Eadie mentions in her book *Embraced by the Light*, we who decide to come to this world are very brave and strong spirits, for not everyone has the courage to face the trials that take place at this level. Acknowledge that you have this merit, and know that you have come to remember the courage that you already came with, through these experiences of fear.

Once you are able to look after yourself in a loving way, you will be able to relate to your loved ones in a healthier way, for dependence will no longer interfere between you.

To develop this responsibility will help you face challenging situations in the future, as well as embracing change more easily.

Identify that fear disguised as benefit, and you will see you can move fast towards your liberation by strengthening your self-esteem.

"It is not the body that gets ill, but the mind."

A Course in Miracles

Symptoms: Why Panic Attacks?

I learned with Louise Hay that our body talks to us; that every symptom it shows is just its way to communicate with us, and make us see something that we are trying to hide. The body is incredibly intelligent and has its own language: symptoms. Each and every one of them is a signal of what is going on internally, and the key to crack their code is to observe which part of the body is affected and the way it is talking. That is where the secret lies.

The complete list is wonderfully compiled in Louise's book, thanks to her years of observation. I will give you just one example: vomit. Let's start by stating which part of the body it is: the digestive system. Its job is to digest, if you'll excuse the repetition. Specifically, it is the stomach the first to receive what we 'ingest'. This is where it all turns very symbolic: what happens when our body takes something and then wants to reject it? We vomit, and it is a very figurative act whenever we cannot accept an idea or a situation that is taking place in our life. Many of you will think: *But what does it mean when I eat something that upsets my stomach? It's the food I had, not some situation that is happening...* Ask yourself: why is it that sometimes something upsets someone's stomach, but then someone else has the exact same thing to eat and had no reaction at all? Could it be that the body of the former was already predisposed to get sick, and all it needed was a trigger? Why is it that some people have the flu while others don't, if it is a virus? What makes your immune system be stronger or weaker? Think about it...

To me it's all about thoughts, the way we assimilate what happens every day; it reflects in our organisms as a way of attracting our attention. Sometimes they are thoughts and very unconscious reactions; things we hid under the rug but that are there, waiting for the perfect moment to come out and be solved by us.

The same thing happens with panic crises; for one thing, only some of us suffer from them, not everybody. I realized that it has to do not only with the aspects I talked about in the chapter "How Is It Born?", but also with a sort of confrontation typical of those who are very sensitive to the energies that surround us. We have a very perceptive sensor, and if we can't handle all that stimulation, we feel overwhelmed. We feel we can't control all the information we are receiving at that moment, and we collapse. That is exactly why many of us have trouble going to very crowded places, such as shopping centers or supermarkets.

If you feel that you are a sensitive person, the best thing to do is to work on handling these energies that you perceive without deciding whether they are good or bad.

One technique that might work is repeating to you: *"This is not mine. What I am sensing belongs to someone else."* Picture yourself covered by an energy shield, or ask an angel to protect you from the vibrations of others. While you are in the process of handling these situations, try to fill yourself with love and confidence, instead of fear, for the latter will not help.

Remember that **nothing** can harm you and that being a little more sensitive or "porous" is a gift. We all have the ability to sense other vibrations, to a greater or lesser degree. But some must develop this ability, while others have it innate. Besides, we are all connected energetically, and if we are able to manage this ability in a way that doesn't affect us, we can use it to help others, as we will have a deeper level of compassion and empathy. For instance, if you were able to identify who or which place gives you a feeling of oppression, you can send out prayers and light, and then give it up to God. Let go of the situation so that the feeling of discomfort disappears.

Going back to anxiety crises, you may have realized that not everybody experiences them in the same way. Some feel shortness of breath, others feel dizzy, or a tingling sensation, palpitations, chest tightness, vomiting, nausea... and many other symptoms, with their respective combinations in every person. Observing all these representations in our body, I was wondering *why is it that she vomits and I feel like fainting, if we have the same disorder.* It wasn't until I connected what each symptom represents that I realized that the uncomfortable situation was a reflection of an unconscious emotion. Shortness of breath is a symbol of feeling like choking, overwhelmed: *I can't breathe; these energies are so many, I can't process them together. I feel like I'm choking.* Dizziness, just like Louise says, is fear of death. Nausea and vomiting mean you reject the particular situation you are experiencing on account of fear; many times, fear of change or fear of giving up security. This is the reason why many people vomit when they travel.

I could go on connecting each part of the body with an emotion or belief that a person may have. But discovering what that symptom is trying to tell me, what that part of the body represents, and the way that symptom is shown, is part of the healing process. This way, we work at the root of the issue. Remember that we achieve nothing by trimming the leaves; if we don't work at the root of the plant, the leaves will keep coming out again and again.

The way I advise people to conduct the analysis is to first observe what is going on in the body. Then, ask yourself what part of the body is it, and what its function is; for example, the throat: to swallow. To continue with the example, the next question would be: *what is it that I don't want to "swallow"?* This way, we can start a dialogue with each symptom to work it out from its origin.

So if every time I travel or go to the supermarket I get nauseous, I can take a pill for it, but the most important thing is to talk with the fear underneath, and explain to ourselves that what we fear will not happen, and the need for medication or agents to give us security will disappear on its own.

But then, ¿What do we do with all the information on the origin of our panic crises and the symptoms and all that? ... How do we work at the root of the problem?

"Now faith is the assurance of things hoped for, the conviction of things not seen"

Hebrews 11:1

Faith

Throughout all my personal process with crises, Faith has been my strongest cane of support.

I would like to start by analyzing the wonderful verse mentioned above; it is my everyday companion:

Faith is the assurance, that is, a truth (a certain and clear knowledge about something), that *things hoped for*, things that I wish for to happen, become real. The conviction, which is a deeper level than knowing or bearing a truth, is TO BE CONVINCED, of what?, *of things not seen*. In other words, it is not only to have the certainty, but to believe that what I wish for is a reality, even when I don't see it materialized in this world yet. This applies to all areas, from wanting more money, to a new job, a relationship, a situation being solved, and in this case, healing and health.

In this matter, Wayne Dyer has been my great guide. He has reminded me that we already have all the things that we wish for, we just have to believe, have faith that is so. This way, we connect to that level in which it's already happening. In our case, it would mean having Faith that the panic episodes will go away, for there is nothing to fear, and that we have heavenly protection upon us at all times, even though we may not see it.

Dr. Dyer talks about thinking from the end, and not towards the end; going to that place in which WE ARE ALREADY HEALTHY, since our natural state is health, not sickness. Notice how the body will always look for the way back to its natural state of health; white blood cells fight battles to evacuate visitors; whenever we cut ourselves, the wounds heal without any help almost always. Our body and our Higher Self know that we are actually health, but it is our Ego who makes us believe that it's not so, and then all kinds of symptoms take place, which are evidence of this imbalance. But they are only signs, we never actually stopped being healthy, and we need to focus precisely on what we DON'T SEE but HOPE FOR. Even though the symptoms try to call our attention, and even when they may be all we see at that moment, the answer is to go back to our reality, where we are complete, healthy and plentiful. That is why Wayne Dyer talks about thinking FROM the end; in other words, as if we were already there:

"to envision ourselves in the conditions that we hope for".

Many people ask themselves what they need to do to have faith. Actually, there is nothing that needs to be done to obtain faith: we already have it! We were all endowed with the seed of faith; the Bible calls it a gift. However it was that we obtained it, we all have faith from the moment we are born, and we can witness this every time we breathe. Even though we can't see the oxygen, we know it is there, and we never question whether it's going to be there a few seconds later, the next time we breathe in.

Now, this faith is given to us in the form of seed, and it is our job to sow it in the best soil, to water it every day, to provide it with the sunlight it needs, and basically to watch it carefully while the plant is still small. Once it has reached a good size, we don't need to keep such a close eye on it, for it is strong on its own and it will hardly ever die. The same thing happens with Faith: it may be very fragile when facing external threats, but once its stem becomes a trunk, nothing and no one can pull it off our hearts, not even the fiercest hurricane.

Actually the seed came to my life, literally. I prayed a lot and asked God to give me faith to cope with my panic episodes. I used to lie in my car under my favorite trees (they are large trees, and in March they fill with hundreds of pink and violet flowers). Anyway, I would lie there to think, relax, and dream that one day I would have all those trees in my yard.

One day, when I went back home, I noticed something on the car's dashboard. I picked it up and I realized it was a seed: a seed from one of those trees. I still don't understand how, but it flew and managed to go through my car window and land on the dashboard, instead of a seat or the floor, where it would have been easily ignored or stepped on. A voice inside my head told me to sow it, to call it the Tree of Faith, and that it would grow as long as I looked after it and watered it every day; just like my faith.

I still have my little tree of Faith, waiting to be planted in the huge backyard that I will have some day. I recommend that if you feel this is a method that will help you view your process of Faith in a more real way, then do it: pick a seed and take care of it every day.

If you would rather look at it in a different way, I also like to use the analogy of a gym with this subject. Faith is like exercising; it is an everyday discipline. We can't just go to the gym a few times and expect our muscles to develop completely. It takes time, and the results will not be immediate. This is what I call *Faith weightlifting*; at the beginning you will feel tired and frustrated, but once you have developed the muscles of Faith, you will have the strength that you wanted.

Remember this is a process; it is something you need to develop. As it grows, it becomes stronger, until it becomes a part of your daily thoughts and actions.

There will be a time in which you will live in Faith every day without any effort, with the certainty that all that we hope for already exists, even when we may not see it, and that the protection from God and His angels will always surround us. Besides, no one has ever died from a panic attack. Our Faith must be placed in health, not in sickness.

Faith can be theoretical or applied, and that is up to you. Many people know exactly what Faith is about and how to ask for it, but when it comes to putting it into practice, all of their theory is useless. We may have passed the theoretical courses on Faith, but it is useless if we can't apply it when the practical courses come. That is when our Faith is really measured. If we face a challenging situation and all the obstacles seem to indicate that what we want doesn't exist, that's when our Faith must be put into practice. Whether it is a financial situation reflecting shortage, doors being closed before us, nervous breakdown after nervous breakdown, disease, low grades in school; whatever the challenge may be, we must always make an effort to remember that we already have what we asked for. Remember what 1 John 5:15 says (see chapter 3).

Not only do we already have what we asked for, but we never actually *stopped having* it. Health has always been there, peace and calm have always been inside of us, but we forget it.

It's time to move to the practical level of Faith, and do all those things that you are so afraid of, with the confidence that everything will be alright. *Act as if* there were no more panic episodes for the day, for the week, for the month.

Act as if there was money already in your bank accounts, as if you already were with that person you want, and you will see that confidence and security lie actually within you, regardless of what happens on the outside.

Go and do your shopping in peace, even when you're only able to do it for a few minutes. Shop a little and then come back later for the rest. Go watch only half a movie, who cares? The important thing is that you realize that nothing wrong is going to happen, and as your confidence grows, the time in which you are able to do the things that you're so afraid of will also increase.

The secret is to have confidence. Reassure yourself that nothing bad is going to happen, even though you don't believe at first. Just like Iyanla Vanzant says, "fake it 'til you make it".

Remember that no one has ever died from a panic attack, no one! Basically, it is uncomfortable and annoying, but since we know that it's not dangerous, we can take away the power that it has over our lives and it will slowly disappear by itself.

And Jesus said: "Go; let it be done for you as you have believed"
Matthew 8:13

"During the time of the darkest night, act as if the morning has already come."

The Talmud

You Are the Only One Who Will Always Be There

As I mentioned before, panic crises have to do with feelings of abandonment and lack of protection that we carry from our childhood. That is why we easily cling to people or situations that make us feel safe, however illusory it may be. For some, it may be their mother, or a job, or their partner, or a certain economic level, or a neighbor, or their house, or some geographical location… either way, our inner child is desperately looking for something to cling onto that seems secure, and develops a dependency. Therefore, every time the person feels that "security object" is missing, he or she will feel again that old abandonment that had been swept under the rug all those years ago, and the panic attack arises.

The thing is, nothing is certain in this world we live in: people become distant or die, couples separate from one another, jobs come to an end, the world economy may change... therefore our peace and happiness cannot depend on external situations, for as we have seen they don't last forever. They can even be momentary circumstances; for instance, when I experienced an anxiety episode, I used to call my mother, but it turned out my mother couldn't always come to the phone. Sometimes she would be in the bathroom, or maybe taking another phone call, and even though she intended to always be there for me in those moments, sometimes she simply couldn't, and I had to calm myself down.

This is precisely where this chapter's title makes sense, for there are only two people whom we can always count on: God and ourselves! It sounds silly, but that's the way it is. You are the only one who will always be there with you, and this is why we must change our dependency on the external to start depending only on the internal.

This is where we can pick up what we left pending at the end of Chapter 2, when I mentioned that we carry a scared little child within us. The moment we understand that nothing external can heal us, then we will stop looking for someone to take care of us, to comfort and calm us down like we wish they had in our childhood. From our adolescence onwards, we become our own parents; if we expect someone else to do so, we will probably experience disappointment, and the suffering will go on even more.

That little child needs a parent, and only you can be that for him or her. We won't let that child trust again in someone who we are not sure is going to be there always. It has to be someone we can be sure of; that *someone* is God and you. I assure you that you will be there with yourself every single day of your life, and that you can tell yourself the exact same words of comfort that your mother or your therapist tells you. In those moments of despair, all that child needs is a hug, and to hear that everything will be fine, that s/he is not alone, and that you will be there in this moment of anguish. Those warm words that we all want to hear have to come out of you now, and it doesn't mean that we shouldn't hear them at all from anyone else; it means that we shouldn't depend on someone else to say them for us to feel secure again.

Picture this scene: you are about to have surgery. From the moment you realized you were going to a hospital, your anxiety levels have been very high. Your mother has been by your side at all times, comforting you. However, the time comes, and the nurses take you to the operating room, and no relatives are allowed beyond those automatic doors. If you depend on your mother, those will be the most distressing seconds of your life.

I don't mean to be a fatalist, and many of you will never have to live an experience like this; I wanted to illustrate the idea that we can only count on ourselves for sure, so when it comes to depending, let's depend on something that we know will always be there for certain.

Many people find it very positive to get a picture of when they were children and imagine that little person right next to them, whenever they are happy or scared, and talk to their inner child. This way, they become their own parent.

Some of us find it easier to *"give ourselves some therapy"* or have a conversation with ourselves, picturing ourselves as we are currently: from one adult to another, as if we were talking to a friend who is going through a moment of anguish. For other people, these feelings of care or protection come out more naturally with pets, so they can picture themselves as a puppy or a little cat who is scared and abandoned, and that only they can calm down.

Regardless of the image that works best for you, the important thing is that we let that loving adult come out and tell us exactly what we wanted to hear when we were children. By doing this, whatever the words we use, we will be filled with love and serenity. In other words, we will reconnect with our source, where everything is fine, and everything will always be fine, because nothing else exists.

In short, let us learn to keep ourselves company at all times, in order to strengthen and empower that little boy or girl that we carry within, and that still feels abandoned; because, as people say, feelings that are buried alive never die.

That feeling of being unprotected will eventually transform into confidence and Faith, and doubt will never have a place in our minds again, for where there is love, there is no place for fear.

Once that little boy or girl walks with security by our side, it will be like when Neo asks his guide in the movie *The Matrix*:

Neo: —What are you trying to tell me? That I can dodge bullets?

Morpheus: —No, Neo. I'm trying to tell you that when you're ready, you won't have to.

In other words, it's not that one day we will be able to avoid panic crises, or "dodge them" in some way. One day we will realize that they actually don't even exist; that it's our mind making us believe that the threat is real.

I see the process of change as if we were put in a maze:

The first couple of times we find it very difficult, because if we go down the wrong way (or when we have a panic episode), we have to go back to the starting point. We must go over all that we have learned about how to act when we let the episodes happen.

The strategy is to learn from these small crises, and then every time they "send us back to the starting point", we will go quicker over the part that we walked before we get to the obstacle that stopped us the last time. Until, eventually, it doesn't bother us to start over and walk through all that section again... we will do it in a matter of seconds.

I like to use this image to explain that, even though we feel that each panic episode takes us back to where we started, the important thing is to remember that we can learn to handle them, and every time we experience an episode, we will remember what we did the last time to get out of the maze.

With time, you let go of your fear for the episodes, and you will be OK with going back to the starting point of the maze, for you already know what to do and you will be able to do it in a matter of minutes, and later in a matter of seconds, until you don't have to pass through that maze, for confidence has taken the place that fear used to have.

Going back to our example from the movie *The Matrix*, all those times we go through the maze it will be like dodging bullets, but once Faith has been installed within us and we take back the power that we had given to the moments of panic, we will comprehend that the bullets exist only if we want them to.

Light casts out darkness.

"And we know that all things work together for good to those who love God."

Romans 8:28

Finding the Blessings in Every Situation

Even when everything looks dark in moments of crisis, there are always blessings waiting to be discovered; the whole experience of enduring the panic attacks opens doors for us to make big changes in our lives. Depending on the way we take it, it can become a purifying path that will make us pass through the fire like gold, but at the end it will make us shine in the purest way.

Personally, I believe that one of the biggest lessons in life is to love ourselves, and this is related to the previous chapter, for when we accept that child with his or her complexes and grieves, we will be able to forgive ourselves; this is the only way we can reach love.

If a disease or an obstacle leads us to self-love, I call it a blessing.

Many people must deal face to face with a terminal disease, or some serious and complex condition, to realize who they really are. But it doesn't have to be that way: it is our decision to take the long, rough road.

Those of us who chose the road of panic attacks must align our thoughts, but nothing more, because our bodies remain intact, while others decide to work on their healing while they struggle with some disease in their bodies. That is why when people complain about panic moments, I remind them of this, for it is much easier to deal with panic attacks than to deal with cancer.

I found more than acceptance that night that I described in the Introduction. While I was coiled up around my pillow, I could only think that this had to happen for a reason, that there had to be a purpose behind this inexplicable suffering; in that moment, I started picturing myself giving talks and lectures in front of many people, and I heard myself saying: *if I survived those nights, you can too!* It was then that I understood that I had to pass through these crises in order to really comprehend my patients or anyone experiencing the same situation. I convinced myself that it was necessary to experience the same things they were feeling to be able to say with conviction: *I know exactly what a panic attack is like!* For the first time in hours, I smiled, in spite of the tears that kept coming out. I could smile because I knew that I had to survive that night, because I had a mission with all those people, because no one understands better than a person who has been through the same thing. That is why all the leaders of Alcoholics Anonymous, Narcotics Anonymous, groups of abused people and others, are individuals that have also suffered from those situations. Who better to understand us in our pain than someone who has also suffered from it?

Thanks to this experience, I started to walk my spiritual path and I became closer to God. I changed my lifestyle and my diet for a healthier one. I took up my gifts again, the gifts that I had discovered as a little girl but I had put away as a grownup, when I thought them to be foolish or mere things that I made up. I even moved away from some people that didn't agree with my new way of living; others came to me with similar ways of thinking to mine.

One circumstance led to another, and it was like finding a chest with an endless treasure, for each day I receive new wisdom in the form of books, songs, phrases, movies, persons.

I learned to seek peace and love above all, and the rest fell on its own. I have even lost my fear of death, little by little, and that has driven my anxiety episodes away. Now I believe in all those beautiful stories of people who have died and come back with their message.

Each one of you also receives blessings with every difficult situation in your lives. I would say, without a doubt, that the first one would be compassion, and it is no coincidence that Jesus talked to us so much about it. Because being able to really understand others, and putting oneself in their shoes, is one of the greatest feelings that we can experience; that is the only way we can accept and love somebody. How powerful to be able to fulfill the commandment of Jesus: love one another! It is repeated in the Bible several times for a reason.

The blessings will be diverse for each one of us, because we all come with a list of things we must learn, custom-made for each and every one. Compassion is just the first of many.

God is so wonderful that He doesn't just give us blessings; there are also blessings for the people who surround us, for they are not there by accident. If they are there and participate in our crises, it is because they have something to learn as well. Therefore, not only are we apprentices, but also instruments for others to grow spiritually. Just to think of this makes me feel amazed.

If you manage to polish your spiritual lenses, you will be able to see all the lessons you can learn and all the positive things that every difficult experience brings to our lives.

To know yourself, to love yourself, to forgive yourself, to change your lifestyle for a better one, to meet other people, to become closer to God, to feel compassion for others, to change old thoughts, to feel calm for the first time in years, to understand that parent that suffered from the same thing you do but was unable to handle it, to help others; all these and many more are the blessings that you can receive if you decide to see them, and most important, to receive them, because they are there. They have always been.

It wasn't until that day that I told you about in the Introduction that I could understand one of the greatest blessings of my panic attacks. That night I survived, and guess what... today I can say that I know exactly how you feel; but if I could, then you can too!

"Meditation is the only means to the harmonious development of the body, mind, and soul."

Maharishi Mahesh Yogi

Techniques

In this chapter, I will present some of the many techniques that have worked for me and for the participants in the support group that I conduct. In any case, not all the techniques work for all of us, so you can take the ones that will work, modify them, give them your own personal style, and even create new ones. Actually, that's how I've discovered most of my techniques: through intuition and paying attention, because the solution I was looking for may be in the simplest, most ordinary things.

Meditation:

This is one of the most ancient techniques, and it works not only for panic attacks. At the beginning I was a little skeptical about meditation. I thought: *how can something so simple do so much?* Soon enough,

I changed my mind when I saw the changes that were taking place in me. I felt calmer during the day; I could enjoy every moment of the day, even in the middle of traffic in the city. I felt more love for everything and everyone; all this with just a few minutes of meditation every night.

For Buddhists, meditation means "*to remain effortlessly* in what is". They say that meditation is an internal practice that allows us to connect in a direct way to the "mind" itself; it is the essential condition to grow in wisdom and eradicate the suffering.

Meditation calms the mind down, and allows the present to finally happen in our lives. It helps us connect with our source, just like A Course in Miracles says:

"His Voice awaits your silence, for His Word cannot be heard until your mind is quiet for a while."

It also lifts our vibrations, and this gives us a high potential of expression.

There are many types of meditation, so may you choose the one you like the most and the one that best works for you.

Visualization:

This is one of my favorite techniques, and one of the most used by the people that I work with. It should be noted that, contrary to what many people think, visualization and meditation are two different things.

Visualization consists of creating images, sounds, flavors, and sensations in a state of "waking dream".

It works therapeutically for all types of difficulties, such as mourning, stress, and anxiety, expressing in the material world, letting out anger or grief, talking to people or beings we can't see, such as angels or loved ones that have passed away. In short, it can be used for anything you want, for the field of the mind is endless.

I always advise those who attend the groups that I conduct to do a relaxing visualization before going to sleep, with landscapes that fill them with peace inside, and if they feel stressed or worried, I suggest they include the image of Jesus or an angel walking towards them with a small box. They place all their worries inside this box, and that spirit of light takes it away. The important thing is to **really** let go of the load, as we may unconsciously fail to hand it over, so the anxiety won't go away. The key is to have confidence that the universe or God is taking care of this situation; therefore, we can give ourselves permission to experience peace and relaxation.

The phrase "Let go and let God..." connects several subjects analyzed in previous chapters, such as control, faith, and the story of the restaurant. But I want to mention them again because in order to really achieve peace, we have the choice of having full confidence in those situations over which we have no control, which is basically everything outside of ourselves. Believing that everything is resolved, and

Silvia Araya

that whatever the outcome of any situation, we will be fine because God is in charge.

Breathe:

One thing that the two previous techniques have in common is deep breathing.

Breathing in intensely a few times will oxygenate our whole body, relax our muscles, and slow down the rhythm of our heartbeat.

The advantage of this exercise is that we can do it wherever we are, sitting down or standing up, whether we are surrounded by a few or a lot of people.

During a panic episode, respiration is the first thing that is affected. Therefore, it is important to return it back to its natural state, and the rest of the organism will follow.

Combine respiration with meditation or visualization to achieve an even higher state of relaxation.

Breathe abundantly while you remember that everything is fine, and that you are protected always.

You may include this habit in your daily routine, even when you are not experiencing a nervous moment.

Thought-Emotion:

Even though panic attacks occur unexpectedly and grow fast at the moment of crisis, if we pay close attention to what happens inside our head at that moment, we will be able to discover a staggered pattern that goes more or less like this:

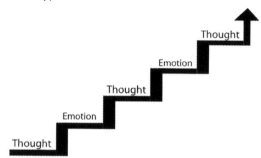

There is an initial thought, for instance:

—*What if I had a heart attack here, in this bus? No one would be able to help me. We're in the middle of nowhere and nobody knows me.*—

Almost immediately, we would start to feel pain in our chest (Reaction).

We think: —*My chest hurts. That's one of the first signs.*

Next, our left arm starts to tingle (Reaction).

We think: — *Of course! It is a heart attack, I'm just missing...*

Then we feel nauseous, and we think: — *That's it! It IS a heart attack. Last week I saw on the Discovery Channel that chest pain, tingling of the arm and nausea are all symptoms of a heart attack.*

It may sound funny, but many situations like this happen in our mind, in a matter of seconds, and when we realize it, we are at the height of the crisis, with very little control over ourselves.

At the height of the crisis, it may not be impossible but it certainly is more difficult to calm down. The trick here is to stop the situation from escalating as soon as possible, and the key moments to do so are whenever a thought comes to mind; that is why I underlined them in the figure.

The sooner we change our thoughts, the faster we will stop the escalation. So whenever you see a catastrophic thought come to your mind, whatever the context is, change it for a thought that brings you closer to love, not fear.

Following the same example of the bus:

—*What if I had a heart attack here, in this bus? No one would be able to help me. We're in the middle of nowhere and nobody knows me.*

The chest pain starts (Reaction).

Let's change that thought to: —*As I know myself good enough, I know that this pain in my chest is not due to a heart attack, but to a panic attack.*

Another option could be: —*If I take this bus every day and never have a heart attack, what makes me think I will have one today?*

Or also: —*God* (or however you want to call him) *is with me. He said He would never abandon me, and that He would send his angels always. So I will not fear, for help will be here when I need it, although today is not the case.*

You can create many other versions of this internal dialogue. The point is we need to change every thought that comes, so that the reaction may change as well. Remember that the mind can't distinguish what is real from what is not, and the body only follows the mind's instructions. But since you do know the difference, you can change the direction anytime. The sooner the better!

Be gentle with yourself:

During the whole healing process, remember to always be gentle with yourself. Judging and mistreating yourself will only slow down the way. A child understands better with love than with scolding. Whenever you engage in this kind of behavior, stop and close your eyes. Picture how you felt as a child when they told you negative things. If you can't picture yourself, then imagine any other child being mistreated like that, because s/he doesn't know how to face the obstacles yet. As a grownup, you know how to face them, and you can teach him/her in a loving way.

Keep in mind that you are always doing the best that you can at all times, according to the knowledge and the tools that you possess. If you don't have them, then it may not be the time to take that next step just yet.

Be patient with yourself, because when you make changes many things are happening within you, and quitting a habit takes time. Give yourself space for the mourning process of your old way of seeing life.

Do not pressure yourself when facing your fears; this may result in more aversion to them. Face your fears when you feel prepared, and in the amount that you feel comfortable with. Many experts recommend facing the feared situation immediately and completely. However, from my experience and the one of those with whom I work, I have realized it is better to first strengthen the inner child and yourself as a loving grownup, and then expose him/her.

Once you have faced the feared situation, feel free to reward your inner child with some activity or food that you like. Every time you overcome a challenging situation, s/he will associate it with a good experience, and you will lose fear insofar as the idea that nothing is going to happen if you ride a bus (or go to the supermarket or the shopping center) burns in your brain.

In our mind, all these scenarios are dangerous and represent a threat. The idea is to change the way we see them and create a new mental impression, as we experience once and again (in a loving, confident way) that there is no danger, and that there never was any.

These connections in the brain are reinforced by either fear or security, depending on what we decide in regards to a particular place or situation. If we want to change, we need to face those places and situations once and again, in order to make our confidence stronger little by little.

This way, you will see how you face your fears gradually and smoothly, without even realizing it. Remember the quote by Vivekananda on chapter 3: lead your efforts to making love and confidence grow within you, and the fear will disappear little by little. It's like turning on the light in a dark room. The light never pushes the darkness away; the darkness retreats on its own in the presence of the divine.

Make peace:

Before you go on cultivating anger and resentment within you, make peace with your panic crises (I know it sounds crazy, but it works). Let us honor any situation or disease that we carry inside; give thanks to it for everything that it has taught you. Apologize to it for blaming it for many of the decisions that you made using it as an excuse.

Talk to your crisis, sit it right next to you with a cup of tea, and tell it that you're sorry. Cry with it, and most important, send it love and light every time it appears, as this will fill you with love and light, and that is like getting a shot of medication. Remember that where there is love, there is no place for fear.

Watch your words:

Words are energy, because they vibrate in the air and they are a reflection of our thoughts and emotions. For decades, Louise has taught us how to use words in our favor, as declarations of what we hope for in our lives. Choose the words that come out of your mouth; that they may be in accordance with health, happiness, and prosperity. Repeat "I am healthy", and you will be.

It is important to say the phrases in the present tense, not in the future, because it is here and now that we want to express our desire, and so we acknowledge that we live in an eternal present.

Personally I've felt that the statement "I Am" is one of the most powerful ones. *I Am Light, I Am Love, I Am Health, I Am Happiness…* You can add in all the words that make you feel better.

On the other hand, check and see how many times in a day you use the phrase "I Am" followed by words such as *dumb, useless, allergic, irritating to other people, depressive, obsessive, abnormal or different from the rest,* and many more that we use every day without realizing it. Imagine what your brain thinks after hearing these phrases once and again… It will buy them! The mind ends up thinking that they are true, and will make them real. So let's make sure that what the mind believes is what will really make us feel good, and will take us where we want to be.

Some people get worried when they notice that they are constantly thinking and saying what they don't want in their lives. They fear that all that repetition will eventually attract that cancer or that heart attack that they are so obsessed with.

However, the vibrations of fear are so low that they are not strong enough to express. On the other hand, the energies of calm, peace and confidence are more effective.

Furthermore, we attract what we are, therefore the only thing you will do is reproduce more fear, because that is the place that you are in at that moment.

Focus on what you desire, not what you want to drive away.

Serving others:

Finally, serving others is as beneficial for the recipient as much as it is for the giver. We all come to serve life one way or the other. Some feel the calling to help children; others, to help young people or the elderly. Some people even dedicate their lives to looking after our plants and animals.

Inside every one of us, our soul longs to serve others, even if it's only by sending light and love from where we are sitting.

However, it can be healing for many, because it places us in a higher vibration and forces us to stop thinking about ourselves and start focusing on others.

Many times, we find ourselves locked up inside our own dilemmas, thinking over and over about the "problem that we suffer from", and ironically this only creates more anxiety, which in turn may lead to a panic crisis.

If we don't stop thinking the matter over for a moment, we are not giving the universe a chance to resolve it. In other words, "we get into God's kitchen", and our fear and worrying keep the miracle from happening.

If we use all that energy in helping another living being, we are saying we trust. To me, it is a perfect technique for any condition, especially depression or panic attacks.

Look around your community for some center or shelter that needs volunteers. If you don't have much time, go at least one hour a week. Even when it may be very little for you, it is a lot for them.

Try it, and you'll see how satisfied you will feel at the end of the day from helping another living being, and how relieved you will be when you stop thinking so much about what you're suffering and what you're "missing".

Final Notes

In this small book, I have written about the advice that has helped me personally as well as all the people that I have been able to counsel. I am aware, however, that not all the recipes work for everybody. Those methods that turn out to be effective for some may not be so for others.

This is why I encourage you to embark on the journey of knowing yourself and knowing your panic crises, as each one of us experiences them in a different way. From this deep knowledge, inspiration and creativity may arise to help you come up with your own techniques to face each episode in a more efficient way, and –why not? – even in a fun way.

Experiment with your own ideas, use situations or hobbies that you like and turn them into your allies. I frequently lean on song lyrics, or inspiring quotes from movies. And just as I have received all that wisdom, so can you if you dispose yourself towards the messages that the universe lays for us everywhere.

When we are open to life, the masters appear; the books, the songs, the quotes, and the methods that will help us on the way. If they don't, we will eventually get the image that will give us ideas to create ourselves the techniques that will work the best in our journey.

Practice the religion that best helps you. Trust life; trust the universe, the space, God, the source. Call your favorite angels and archangels to your side; or millennial masters, saints or ancestors. The important thing is to become aware that you are not alone.

Find the books, the teachings and the techniques that work the best to fill you with peace. There are many different approaches for panic attacks, and they are all equally worthy.

And above all, don't forget that each one of us comes with a toolbox to deal with life's challenges, and this is not the exception. I believe in your potential to discover the person that you really are. Why? Because I didn't believe it of myself, and now I have total confidence in me.

Blessings,

Silvia